EARTH'S ROCKY PAST

METAMORPHIC ROCKS

Richard Spilsbury

PowerKiDS
press™

New York

Published in 2016 by **The Rosen Publishing Group**
29 East 21st Street, New York, NY 10010

Produced for Rosen by Calcium

Editors for Calcium: Sarah Eason and Harriet McGregor
Designers: Paul Myerscough and Jessica Moon
Illustrator: Venetia Dean

Picture credits: Cover: Dreamstime: Les Palenik. Inside: Dreamstime: 12b, Andreanita 22,
Andreus 10–11, Artx 7b, Daveallenphoto 25r, Gelyngfjell 23, Lornet 17r, Aaron Norris 18, Les
Palenik 19t, Douglas Raphael 16–17, Anthony Aneese Totah Jr 19b, David Woods 25l, Peng
Zhuang 8; Shutterstock: Artography 1, 27, Everything Possible 9r, Imfoto 11br, Gail Johnson
15, Les Palenik 5t, Lukiyanova Natalia/Frenta 6, Mopic 20–21, Nito 14t, Fedorov Oleksiy 9l,
Wuttichok Painichiwarapun 14–15, Fedor Selivanov 24, Siim Sepp 5b, 20t, Matthijs Wetterauw
26, Mark Yarchoan 7t; Wikimedia Commons: 13, Brocken Inaglory 12t, NotFromUtrecht 4.

Library of Congress Cataloging-in-Publication Data
Spilsbury, Richard.
Metamorphic rocks / by Richard Spilsbury.
p. cm. — (Earth's rocky past)
Includes index.
ISBN 978-1-4994-0825-6 (pbk.)
ISBN 978-1-4994-0824-9 (6 pack)
ISBN 978-1-4994-0823-2 (library binding)
1. Metamorphic rocks — Juvenile literature.
I. Spilsbury, Richard, 1963-. II. Title.
QE475.A2 S65 2016
552'.4—d23

Manufactured in the United States of America
CPSIA Compliance Information: Batch WS15PK: For Further Information contact Rosen Publishing, New York, New York at 1-800-237-9932

CONTENTS

METAMORPHIC ROCK

Slate and marble are useful and beautiful rocks. You may have seen them on or in buildings. They are examples of metamorphic rocks. Metamorphic means a change in form. Metamorphic rocks change from one rock type into another type.

The famous Leaning Tower of Pisa, Italy, is made from marble. Marble is a metamorphic rock.

ROCKS EVERYWHERE

A huge variety of rocks cover the surface of our planet, forming everything from mountains to **valleys**. All rocks have something in common because they are made from raw materials called **minerals**. Minerals include calcite, **quartz**, and mica. Each mineral is made from one or more kinds of **elements**.

CHANGING ROCKS

Rocks at Earth's surface are very hard because the minerals inside them are solid. Beneath Earth's surface, nearer to Earth's core, it is very hot. Rocks that are near to the core are heated up. They are also squashed by the weight of other rocks above and around them. **Pressure** and heat change the minerals in rocks. The rocks **transform**, or change, into another kind of rock.

striped metamorphic rocks

Clues to the Past

Metamorphic rocks often look different from the rocks from which they formed because they contain different minerals. However, they are still made up of the same elements as the original rock. The elements in metamorphic rocks give us clues about the kinds of rocks they once were.

Metamorphic rocks can look like rocks melted and squashed together.

ROCK STAR STORIES

The oldest known rock on Earth is the Nuvvuagittuq Greenstone Belt in Canada. This large area of metamorphic rock contains minerals that scientists have used to figure out when the rocks were first formed. They think that the Belt could be 4.3 billion years old!

SHIFTING EARTH

A mystery surrounds metamorphic rocks: how did they move underground? The answer lies in the structure of our planet. Although Earth's surface remains mostly still, deep underground rocks are constantly moving.

Earth's layers

OUR PLANET'S LAYERS
Earth has three main parts.

Crust: This is the outer part of our planet, on which we live. It is up to 44 miles (70 km) thick and is broken up into enormous sections, called plates.

Mantle: This solid layer moves around and is about 1,800 miles (2,900 km) thick. Earth's plates float on the hotter, lower part of the mantle.

Core: This is the hottest part of our planet and it forms the center of the Earth.

PLATE *VS.* PLATE
The most incredible **collisions** on Earth happen at the places where Earth's plates meet. Some plates collide in slow motion. When this happens, the edges of the plates

can crumple into giant mountains. When the plates slide against each other, the action causes **earthquakes**. Some plates dip beneath each other, carrying the rocks above them underground. This is how rocks are carried beneath Earth's crust, where they change into metamorphic rocks.

lava

Clues to the Past

Volcanoes form in places where plates are moving apart or where there are gaps in the plates. At these places, molten rock, called magma, comes to the surface. Now known as lava, it cools, forming brand new rock, called **igneous rock**.

The Himalayan **mountain range** contains the highest mountains on Earth. It is made from more than 100 mountains that are all taller than 24,000 feet (7,300 m). The range includes the tallest mountain on Earth, Mt. Everest. The Himalayan range is also one of the youngest mountain ranges on Earth. It formed 50 million years ago when two plates collided and forced rock upward into the mountain range we see today.

ROCK STAR STORIES

the Himalayas

UNDERGROUND ROCK FACTORY

Many miles beneath the ground, conditions are very different from those on Earth's surface. It is much hotter and the pressure is greater. It is these conditions that create new rocks from existing minerals.

Hot, underground rocks heat water.

HEATING UP

Did you know that ice stays frozen around 32° F (0° C), but melts as it gets warmer? The same process takes place with minerals, but at far higher temperatures. The farther a rock travels beneath Earth's surface, the hotter it becomes. This is because it is closer to Earth's incredibly hot core. Near Earth's hot center, rock melts and changes form.

UNDER PRESSURE

Pressure is measured in bars. The pressure on our bodies at Earth's surface is the downward push of the **atmosphere** above our heads. This measures 1 bar. About 20 miles (32 km) underground the pressure measures an incredible 10,000 bars. This huge pressure is created by the downward push of the heavy rock on Earth's surface. Pressure can make the minerals in rocks change.

Some marble contains **fossils**, which are the remains of ancient living things. Fossils are usually found in **sedimentary rocks**. These rocks form when layers of rock or fragments of shells build up, press together, and turn to rock. However, sedimentary rock, like igneous rock, can turn into metamorphic rock at high pressures and temperatures.

ROCK STAR STORIES

If you transported a pencil 100 miles (160 km) underground in a piece of rock, the pressure would be great enough to turn the pencil's lead into diamond! Pencil lead is made from graphite, which contains only the element carbon. At 50–100,000 bars, the arrangement of the carbon pieces in graphite changes, turning it into hard, valuable diamond!

graphite pencil

diamonds

PRESSURE POINTS

If you dive down into a swimming pool, you can often feel your ears pop. This is the effect of pressure on your eardrums. Depth and pressure also affect how metamorphic rock changes.

ONE DIRECTION

When some rocks are pressed hard in one direction, the minerals inside the rocks change shape. **Granite** is an igneous rock with a lot of small minerals spread through it. When pushed from one direction, all the minerals inside the rock line up and point at **right angles** to the push. This creates a new rock. The new metamorphic rock is called **gneiss**.

TRAVELING AND CHANGING

When one area of crust dips beneath another, it can keep traveling deeper. As the rocks in the area of crust gradually move deeper, they change into different kinds of metamorphic rocks. Around 6 miles (9.5 km) deep, a sedimentary rock called shale turns to a metamorphic rock called phyllite. Deeper and hotter still, the phyllite changes into garnet-micaschist. This is a gray rock studded with dark-red **crystals**. At around 14 miles (22.5 km) deep, garnet-micaschist turns into gneiss. Even deeper still, the rock changes to another metamorphic rock called migmatite.

One plate dips beneath the other.

Rocks travel deeper beneath the surface.

Clues to the Past

Some minerals, such as chlorite and muscovite, are formed only at low temperatures and pressures. Others, such as garnet and sillimanite, require great heat and pressure to form. By studying the minerals of metamorphic rocks, scientists can figure out their history.

garnet

HOT WATER

A sugar cube **dissolves** faster in boiling water than cold water. In the same way, the minerals in some rocks in Earth's crust change quickly when they are touched by hot water. This process often happens on ocean floors and creates metamorphic rocks.

HOW WATER GETS IN

One of the places where water often gets deep into Earth's crust is where plates pull apart. Seawater moves down cracks made in rock as the plates pull away from one another. As the water travels deeper inside the crack, and closer to Earth's core, it gets hotter. The very hot water can dissolve minerals and cause **chemical changes** in rocks. For example, hot water that gets into tiny cracks in granite can dissolve minerals rich in iron. It makes red metamorphic rock along these cracks because a new mineral called hematite forms there.

The reddish colors in the Grand Canyon wall are iron-rich metamorphic minerals.

Water entered a crack and changed this rock.

DEEP-OCEAN CHIMNEYS

Dotted along the deep ocean floor are strange chimneys. They form naturally around **vents** (holes) in Earth's crust. High pressure forces hot mineral **solutions** to spurt up through Earth's crust, into the ocean above. When the solutions hit the cold seawater, they cool down. This makes the minerals in the solutions, like copper and iron, turn into crystals. These crystals gradually build up in chimney shapes around the hole in the ocean floor.

The water coming from a deep-ocean chimney looks like smoke because of the enormous numbers of tiny crystals forming there.

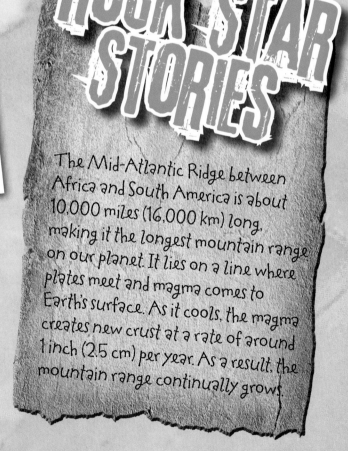

ROCK STAR STORIES

The Mid-Atlantic Ridge between Africa and South America is about 10,000 miles (16,000 km) long, making it the longest mountain range on our planet. It lies on a line where plates meet and magma comes to Earth's surface. As it cools, the magma creates new crust at a rate of around 1 inch (2.5 cm) per year. As a result, the mountain range continually grows.

SLATE

slate

Slate is one of the most popular metamorphic rocks on Earth. This is mostly because it can be easily split. This has made it easy for people to use thin sheets of the rock to waterproof the roofs of buildings.

SHEETS OF CRYSTALS

Slate forms from mud that contains large amounts of clay. When Earth's plates pushed together around 300 to 400 million years ago, the mud was squashed under huge pressure and at high temperatures. Clay contains a mineral called mica. Under pressure, mica forms narrow crystals in sheets at right angles to the direction of the pressure. Slate can be easily broken along gaps between these sheets.

USING SLATE

In a slate mine, people dig out chunks of slate. They use flat chisels and hammers to gently divide the chunk into thinner

thick slate wall

and thinner pieces. Machines cut the slate to different sizes to be used as tiles on roofs. However, slate is not only used on roofs. For example, pool tables often have large sheets of flat slate under their felt so they are always level and the balls roll evenly across the surface of the felt.

DIFFERENT COLORS

Slate comes in different colors depending on the minerals it contains. Dark slate usually contains black iron sulfide, and red slate usually contains hematite. Green slate contains chlorite, which is a green mineral.

ROCK STAR STORIES

The best-quality slate in the world is from Wales in the United Kingdom. Welsh slate is harder, stronger, and longer-lasting than any other slate in the world. Welsh slate was first prized by the Romans and by the late nineteenth century, the two largest slate mines in the world were in Wales. There are few Welsh slate mines today, but their slate is still in high demand.

Welsh slate

MARBLE

Marble is a beautiful rock. This metamorphic rock is hard but is easy to cut. It can also be polished to show off its stunning veins, or lines, and swirling blotches of color.

SEDIMENTARY TO METAMORPHIC

Marble begins life as the sedimentary rock limestone, which contains mostly the mineral calcite. Intense pressure over long periods of time causes the mineral to melt. It then forms multi-shaped, **interlocking** crystals. This makes the marble much harder than the original sedimentary rock. The colors in marble are caused by **impurities** in the crystals.

USING MARBLE

Marble reflects light well because it has a tight crystal structure. This light-reflecting quality means that marble is used for decorative surfaces like kitchen countertops, gravestones, statues, and the surfaces of buildings. One of the most famous marble buildings is the Taj Mahal in India, which was built in the seventeenth century. The building is made from white marble and **precious stones**.

Taj Mahal

Clues to the Past

Most marble forms when plates push into each other. However, some forms when lumps of incredibly hot magma rise up through rock nearer the surface. This bakes the limestone in the rock into marble. Marble formed this way usually has smaller calcite grains than that formed by large movements in Earth's crust.

ROCK STAR STORIES

Michelangelo's David

What do the Peace Monument in Washington, D.C., the Pantheon in Rome, Italy, and Michelangelo's David sculpture in Florence, Italy, all have in common? They are all made from marble dug from Carrara quarry in Tuscany, Italy. Its pure-white or blue-gray veined marble has been prized since Roman times.

GNEISS

One of the most common metamorphic rocks, gneiss, has bands that run through it. The bands in gneiss can be either incredibly obvious or are so small they can be seen only by using a microscope. Whatever the size, the bands tell us how the rock formed.

HIGH-PRESSURE ROCKS

Of all the metamorphic rocks, gneiss has some of the biggest grains. This proves that, like marble, gneiss forms at very high temperatures. At high temperatures, some mineral grains dissolve, making room for other mineral grains to grow bigger. In gneiss, the large mineral grains are also arranged in bands, as this rock forms at very high pressures. The lighter bands are often made of quartz and feldspar minerals.

TYPES OF GNEISS

Gneiss can be identified by the kind of rock from which it formed, the types of minerals it contains, or their shapes. Pencil gneiss has a lot of pencil-shaped minerals running through it. Augen gneiss has mineral lumps that are shaped a little like the lenses of eyes. This is why the rock is called augen, which means eye in German.

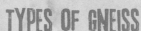
Lines of quartz in gneiss along a river valley.

caption: evenly banded gneiss

Clues to the Past

Just imagine how a stack of pancakes would fold and twist if you pushed it from the side. When gneiss is pushed in one direction, the effect is similar. The bands in gneiss are not always even and may be twisted. This proves that the rock was pushed in the direction of the bands after the bands had been formed.

ROCK STAR STORIES

One of the most famous kinds of gneiss is often called rainbow granite because it has striking colors and is formed from granite. The Morton Gneiss from Minnesota has pink, swirling bands running through it. This 3.5 billion-year-old rock is used as a decorative stone.

caption: rainbow granite

MINERALS

A wide range of minerals can be found in all kinds of rocks. However, some are very unusual and found only in metamorphic rocks.

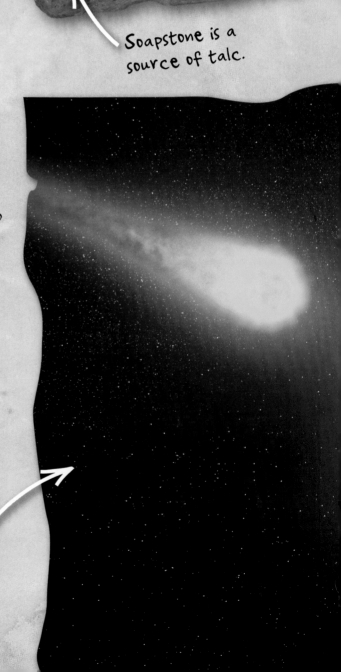

Soapstone is a source of talc.

SUPER-SOFT TALC

Did you know that the talcum powder people sprinkle on themselves after a bath is actually a ground-up mineral taken from metamorphic rock? Soapstone and serpentinite are green-colored rocks formed deep underground that also contain talc. Talc is the softest mineral on Earth, because its layers of silicate crystals are only weakly stuck together. Ground talc absorbs moisture and people use it to help them dry their bodies.

Rocky meteorites occasionally strike Earth, creating rare metamorphic rocks.

DANGEROUS ASBESTOS

Asbestos has unusually long, thin, straight, or curly crystals that are rather like fabric **fibers**. This metamorphic mineral was once used to make materials that can resist heat, like pipes or theater curtains. However, asbestos is rarely used today because it is dangerous to human health. Its very thin, light, sharp fibers can be easily breathed in. They stay in the body and cause damage to the lungs.

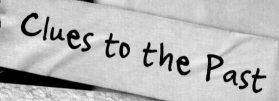

asbestos

Clues to the Past

Suevite is an unusual metamorphic rock that contains shattered stones and glassy minerals. It is rare because it forms only where meteorites from space hit Earth. Meteorites strike at speeds of up to 100,000 miles per hour (160,900 km/h). The collision speed causes rock minerals from both the meteorite and the rock on Earth to melt and break. The rock minerals then cool and reform into suevite. The rock is useful because it tells scientists when and where meteorites hit Earth in the past.

REACHING THE SURFACE

Most metamorphic rocks are formed miles underground. They reach Earth's surface through powerful natural processes. Some are forced to the surface as one plate moves over the top of another. However, many surface as if by magic as part of a process called the **rock cycle**.

WORN AWAY

Surface rock gradually **weathers** or breaks into smaller pieces. For example, when ice freezes in cracks it forces the cracks to grow wider. Rushing rivers, crashing waves, or wild winds can carry or **erode** surface rock pieces away. This gradually reveals the rocks

Harder rock withstands weathering and erosion longer than soft rock, creating spectacular rock formations.

beneath. The speed at which weathering or erosion of rock takes place depends on the softness of the rocks. Hard lumps of rock can remain even when the softer rock that formed around it has gone.

COMPLETING THE CYCLE

The pieces of rock worn away by weathering and erosion can form new sedimentary rock. This rock may eventually become buried deep beneath Earth's surface, where it turns into new metamorphic rocks. These new rocks may themselves become buried even deeper, and eventually their minerals melt to become part of new igneous rock at Earth's surface. The formation and destruction of rocks in this way is Earth's rock cycle.

Wind and water have weathered and eroded this desert rock.

ROCK STAR STORIES

Erosion usually takes place very slowly but it can happen suddenly and with deadly results. In 1970, in Peru, a chunk of ice about 0.6 mile (1 km) across and weighing millions of tons fell off a mountain. It hurtled down a valley, pushing a wall of snow, rock, soil, and ice hundreds of feet high in front of it. It completely buried a town called Yungay, killing thousands of people.

METAMORPHIC WORLDWIDE

Metamorphic rocks can form anywhere on Earth where surface rock becomes buried deep enough beneath the surface to change into metamorphic rock. However, we find most metamorphic rocks in certain places.

WHERE PLATES MEET

Some of the best places to look for metamorphic rocks are where plates meet. The extreme pressure of the collision of two plates, and the push of one plate beneath another, are ideal places for metamorphic rocks to form. There are large areas of metamorphic rocks near mountain ranges, including the Alps, in Europe, and the Himalayas, in Nepal. Both ranges formed when plates buckled into one another millions of years ago.

the Alps, Europe

PRECIOUS ROCKS

Some valuable minerals within metamorphic rock are found in large quantities, or **mineral deposits**, in specific places on Earth. For example, jade is a semi-precious stone that is especially valuable in China, where it is used to make sculptures and ornaments. Today, there is too little jade in Chinese quarries to meet demand for the mineral, so people import (buy in) the mineral from bigger deposits in British Columbia, Canada.

gneiss

Blue Ridge Mountains

The Caledonian Mountains once stretched from Greenland through the United Kingdom and into the United States. They formed when two ancient continents collided around 450 million years ago, as Earth's plates shifted. Much of the top of the Caledonian Mountains has now weathered and eroded, but there are a lot of places where the metamorphic rock that formed when the plates collided have now reached the surface. These include the Blue Ridge Mountains of Virginia, and the Outer Hebrides islands, United Kingdom.

ROCK STAR STORIES

AMAZING METAMORPHIC

Metamorphic rocks are important parts of our planet's surface and provide vital **resources** for humans. Their constant formation deep beneath our feet is the result of powerful natural processes.

This crumpled metamorphic rock gives us clues about Earth's movements in the past.

ROCKS TELL STORIES

Metamorphic rocks are fascinating because their minerals, shapes, and structures are a record of the huge changes going on all the time underground. They show us what the great heat and pressure deep inside our planet can do. Metamorphic rocks reveal how the boiling pot of heat and pressure inside Earth is constantly changing our planet.

Clues to the Past

We can identify different kinds of common metamorphic rocks by asking the following questions:

1. Do they have bands or layers?
   If the answer is yes, the rocks are probably slate (has thin layers), schist, or gneiss (has dark and white bands). If the answer is no, the rocks are probably marble or quartzite.

2. How big are the grains in the rock?
   If they are small, the rock is probably slate. If they are large, it is gneiss or schist.

3. Are the rocks hard enough to scratch glass?
   If the answer is yes, the rock is quartzite, gneiss, or schist. If the answer is no, the rock could be slate or marble.

mixed metamorphic rocks

RUNNING OUT OF ROCKS?

Slate, marble, talc, gneiss, and other metamorphic rocks are important resources for building. The metamorphic rocks that form mountains and cliffs come under threat when people dig up too much stone. Deep-ocean places, where rare creatures live, are under threat because people want to mine the metamorphic minerals near vents. Although new metamorphic rock is forming all the time, this process is very slow. We must not use too much of our planet's precious metamorphic rocks or we will begin to run out.

ROCK YOUR WORLD!

It takes millions of years for metamorphic rock to form from other kinds of rocks. However, you can see the rock-forming process in action much more quickly by mirroring it using chocolate!

YOU WILL NEED:

- plastic knife
- dark and white chocolate bars
- foil paper and foil baking cups
- flat bowl to hold hot water
- hot water from a faucet (ask an adult to help you)

COMPLETE THESE STEPS:

1. Using the knife, shave several pieces from each bar in separate piles.

2. Gather these shavings into layers on a piece of foil paper, fold it over, and press down on the pieces. Open up the foil to reveal your "sedimentary" chocolate.

3. Place a piece of your sedimentary chocolate, some more shavings, and a few chunks from the bars into a baking cup.

4. Float the baking cup in the bowl of hot water.

5. Watch as the heat from the water transfers to the foil and to the chocolate, which should start to melt.

6. Press the plastic knife into the chocolate. If it is soft, remove the baking cup from the water.

7. Let the chocolate cool and, while still soft, push in the sides of the cup.

WHAT HAPPENED?

The partly-melted, cooled, and squashed chocolate is your metamorphic chocolate! The shavings and chunks of different chocolate are a little like the mineral grains in rocks. Just like real rocks, the grains melted together and the soft rock could be pushed into new shapes. The process created something different from the original materials. However, unlike real rock, you can eat the result!

TRY IT OUT!

Mimic crystal formation by adding other candies to the chocolate mix. How do they change as you warm the mixture? Do they harden after partial melting? Why not try to mimic igneous rock formation by melting a mix of different chocolates to create a new chocolate blend?

GLOSSARY

atmosphere The layer of gases around Earth.

chemical changes When one or more substances change into a completely different substance.

collisions When objects strike each other.

crystals Solids made up of regular, repeating arrangements of particles.

dissolves Completely mixes with a liquid.

earthquakes Violent shaking of the Earth at the surface caused by movements deeper within the Earth's crust.

elements The simplest chemical substances, such as iron, carbon, or oxygen.

erode Wear away.

fibers Thin threads, strands, or filaments.

fossils Remains of plants or animals that lived millions of years ago, usually preserved as mineral shapes in rocks.

gneiss Metamorphic rock with large mineral grains formed at high pressures and temperatures.

granite Hard igneous rock containing large crystals.

igneous rock Rock formed when magma (molten rock) cools and sets hard.

impurities Substances found in rocks that are not part of the rock's natural structure or composition.

interlocking When two or more materials are linked together.

meteorites Chunks of rock from space that land on Earth.

mineral deposits Large amounts of naturally occurring mineral material left behind by natural processes.

minerals Solid, naturally occurring substances that make up rocks.

mountain range A series of mountains formed in the same way, often in a line.

precious stones Valuable gems or gemstones that are hard, shiny, and beautiful, like diamond or opal.

pressure Force or weight pushing against something.

quartz A hard and common mineral often found as crystals and in all different kinds of rocks.

resources Useful or valuable materials like minerals needed as a raw material for industry. For example, soil is a vital resource for farming and iron minerals are a vital resource for making steel.

right angles Ninety degree angles.

rock cycle The constant formation, destruction, and recycling of rocks through Earth's crust.

sedimentary rocks Kinds of rocks formed from tiny pieces of rock, plants, or shells of marine animals.

solutions Liquids and the substances that are dissolved in them.

transform To change completely.

valleys Low areas of land between hills.

vents Openings in Earth's crust through which hot gases, water, or magma escape.

weathers When rock is broken down into small pieces by natural processes.

FURTHER READING

BOOKS

Aloian Molly. *What Are Metamorphic Rocks?* (Let's Rock!).
New York, NY: Crabtree Publishing Company, 2010.

Green, Dan. *Scholastic Discover More: Rocks and Minerals*.
New York, NY: Scholastic Reference, 2013.

Oxlade Chris. *Metamorphic Rocks* (Let's Rock). Chicago, IL:
Heinemann-Raintree, 2011.

Tomacek, Steve. *National Geographic Kids Everything Rocks
and Minerals*. Washington, DC: National Geographic
Children's Books, 2011.

WEBSITES

Due to the changing nature of Internet links, PowerKids Press
has developed an online list of websites related to the subject
of this book. This site is updated regularly. Please use this link
to access the list: www.powerkidslinks.com/erp/meta

INDEX